LIBRARY SMARTS

DO YOUR RESEARCH

LISA OWINGS

Lerner Publications Company • Minneapolis

For my husband, who teaches me something new every day

Lerner Publications Company
A division of Lerner Publishing Group, Inc.
241 First Avenue North
Minneapolis, MN 55401 U.S.A.

Website address: www.lernerbooks.com

Library of Congress Cataloging-in-Publication Data

Owings, Lisa.
    Do your research / by Lisa Owings.
       pages   cm. — (Library smarts)
    Includes index.
    ISBN 978–1–4677–1503–4 (lib. bdg. : alk. paper)
    ISBN 978–1–4677–1749–6 (eBook)
    1. Research—Methodology—Juvenile literature. 2. Library research—Juvenile literature. 3. Report writing—Juvenile literature. I. Title.
ZA3080.O95 2014
001.4'2—dc23   2013002302

Manufactured in the United States of America
1 – CG – 7/15/13

TABLE OF CONTENTS

What Is Research?

You already know a lot of things. But there is always more to learn. *Learning* means "finding out things you don't know." It means knowing more about subjects you like. Doing research is a great way to learn. *Doing research* means "gathering **information**."

Ask a Question

Research is about asking questions. What do you want to know? Do you wonder why stars shine? Do you want to know how cars move? Maybe you are not sure what a word means. You can do research to find the answers!

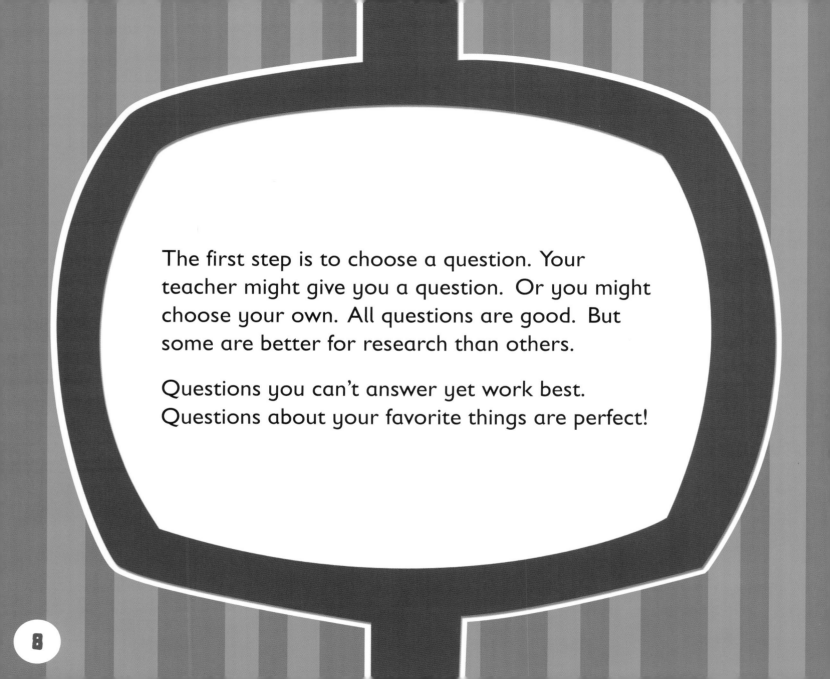

The first step is to choose a question. Your teacher might give you a question. Or you might choose your own. All questions are good. But some are better for research than others.

Questions you can't answer yet work best. Questions about your favorite things are perfect!

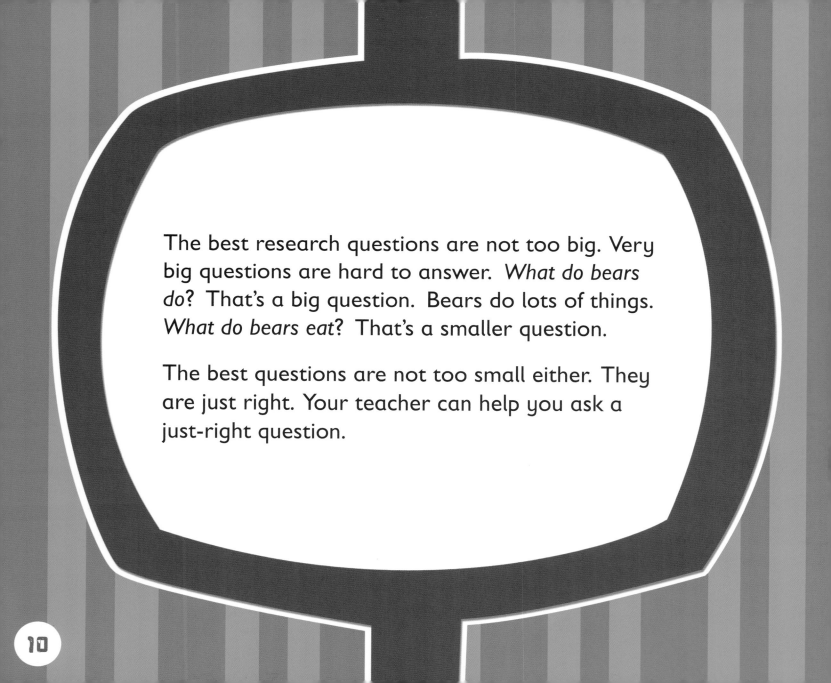

The best research questions are not too big. Very big questions are hard to answer. *What do bears do*? That's a big question. Bears do lots of things. *What do bears eat*? That's a smaller question.

The best questions are not too small either. They are just right. Your teacher can help you ask a just-right question.

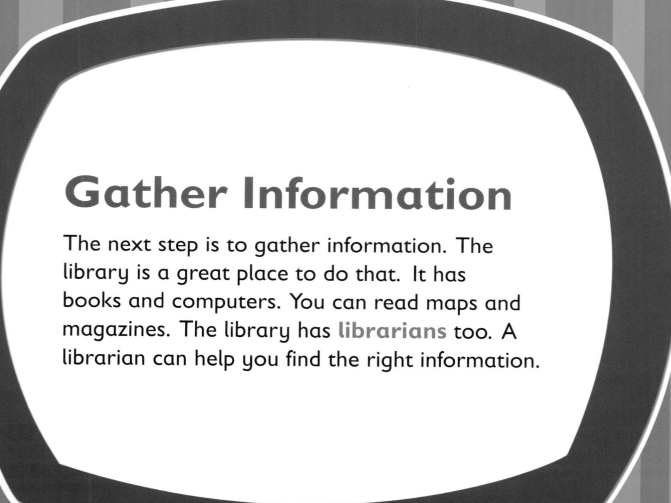

Gather Information

The next step is to gather information. The library is a great place to do that. It has books and computers. You can read maps and magazines. The library has **librarians** too. A librarian can help you find the right information.

Think about your question. What information do you need? Where can you find it? Start with the **library catalog**. A librarian can help.

Check different **sources**. Read books. Go online. Ask your teacher which websites to use. Good sources are true. They are easy to read.

Think about your question. Do your sources help you answer it? Find the **table of contents** in your book. Find the **index**. These tell you where to find information. You can look up what you need. You can also find facts online. A librarian can help you find the best sources.

Table of Contents

Glossary

germs (JURMZ): tiny objects in milk that can cause sickness

teats (TEETS): the parts of a cow that milk flows out of

udder (UH-dur): the part of a cow that makes milk

Index

1. Title.
012010.394

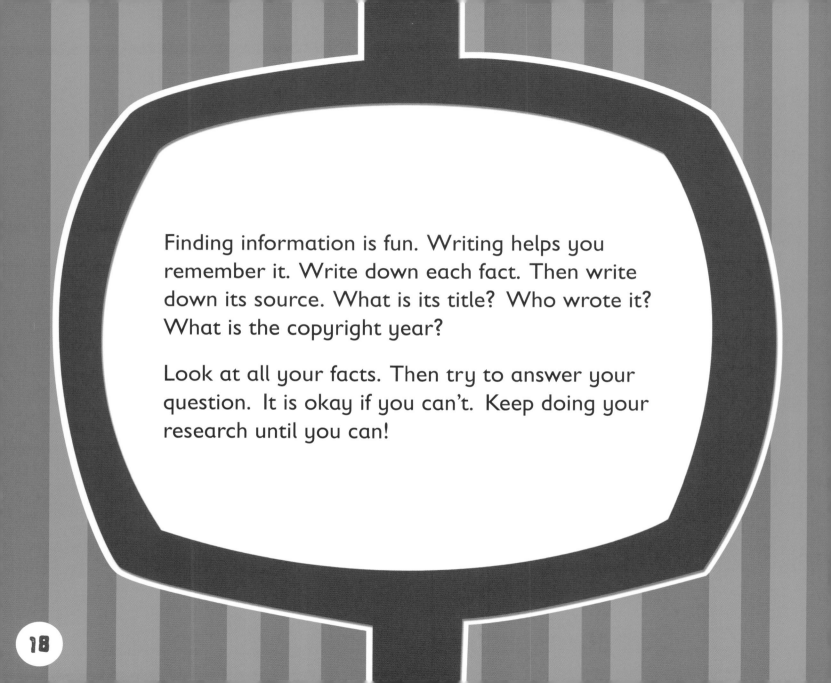

Finding information is fun. Writing helps you remember it. Write down each fact. Then write down its source. What is its title? Who wrote it? What is the copyright year?

Look at all your facts. Then try to answer your question. It is okay if you can't. Keep doing your research until you can!

Works Cited

Frogs. *Kids InfoBits*. Thomson Gale, 2005. Web.

Shannon Zemlicka. *From Tadpole to Frog*. 2012. Print.

Share What You Learned

Have you answered your question? Then it is time to share what you learned! There are many ways to share. Write a report or do a project. Talk to your class or paint a picture. Sharing your research helps others learn too.

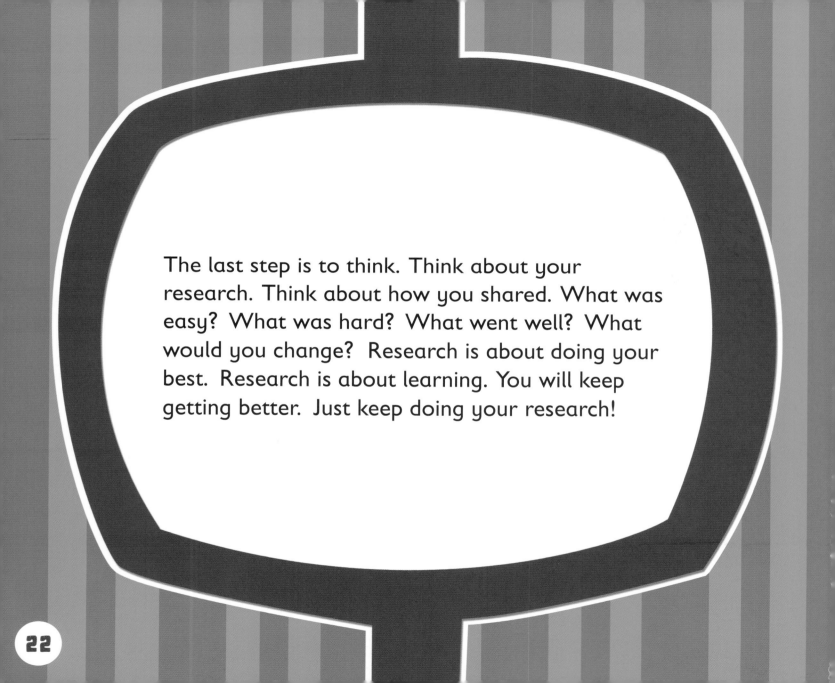

The last step is to think. Think about your research. Think about how you shared. What was easy? What was hard? What went well? What would you change? Research is about doing your best. Research is about learning. You will keep getting better. Just keep doing your research!

GLOSSARY

index: a list of words in alphabetical order, often in the back of a book. It tells where to find information in a book.

information: facts or things you learn by doing research

librarians: people who work in a library

library catalog: a computer tool that tells you about books in the library

sources: things, such as books or websites, that give you information

table of contents: a list of what is in a book, often found at the front of the book. A table of contents shows where to find information.

INDEX

Photo acknowledgments: The images in this book are used with the permission of: © iStockphoto.com/Jani Bryson, p. 5; © Stockbyte Royalty Free, p. 7; © iStockphoto.com/Steve Debenport, p. 9; © iStockphoto.com/Christopher Futcher, p. 11; © Andy Ryan/Taxi/Getty Images, p. 13; © iStockphoto.com/Darren Mower, p. 15; © Todd Strand/Independent Picture Service, pp. 17, 19; © Ryan McVay/Lifesize/Thinkstock, p. 21.

Front cover: © Dmitriy Shironosov/Dreamstime.com.

Main body text set in Gill Sans Infant Std Regular 18/22. Typeface provided by Monotype Typography.